Basil

JANET HAZEN

Illustrations by Pearl Beach

CHRONICLE BOOKS

SAN FRANCISCO

Text Copyright © 1993 by Janet Hazen.
Illustrations Copyright © 1993 by Pearl Beach.
Book Design: Brenda Rae Eno
Calligraphy: Georgia Deaver
Typesetting: Ann Flanagan Typography

Library of Congress Cataloging-in-Publication Data

Hazen, Janet.
    Basil / by Janet Hazen : illustrated by Pearl Beach.
        p.   c.m
    ISBN 0-8118-0170-5
    1. Cookery (Basil)   I. Beach, Pearl.   II. Title.
TX819.B37H37   1993
641.6'57—dc20   92-8772
                                                         CIP

Printed in Hong Kong.

Distributed in Canada by Raincoast Books, 112 East Third Ave.,
Vancouver, B.C. V5T 1C8

10 9 8 7 6 5 4 3 2 1

Chronicle Books
275 Fifth Street
San Francisco, CA 94103

Table of Contents

Introduction   7

A Compendium of Basil   10

Appetizers   17

Soups and Salads   29

Entrées   41

Desserts   57

Index   66

List of Recipes   68

Introduction

asil captures the essence of long summer days filled with radiant sunlight. Its distinctive fragrance and bright, clean taste are unmistakable. One of the world's oldest herbs, basil is native to India, Southeast Asia, and tropical Africa, but it also grows well in the warm climate of the Mediterranean and in some parts of the United States. Most types of basil used for cooking have green leaves, which are highly aromatic and flavorful. The most widely cultivated variety of basil, sweet basil *(Ocimum basilicum),* has bright green leaves, white flowers, and an intense flavor with hints of licorice, mint, clove, and black pepper. With all varieties of basil, the leaves of the plant are used for cooking; the stems are rarely used because they can be tough, fibrous, and bitter tasting.

Like many herbs, basil has been grown for both medicinal and culinary purposes for centuries. Basil was used by ancient Greeks and Romans, who had superstitious sentiments about its properties. The derivation of the word *basil* is from the Greek word *basilikon,* meaning "royal," and the Latin word *basiliscus,* which referred to "basilisk," a mythical fire-breathing dragon. According to Roman legend, basil was an antidote to the venom of the basilisk—a dreaded serpent whose glance and breath were allegedly fatal.

The history of basil in both Europe and the United States is long and diverse; it has graced ornamental gardens, been added to herbal remedies, and become the signature herb of many traditional dishes. The English embraced the herb in the early 1600s, when it began to play an important role in herb gardens. Italy, France, and other European countries incorporated basil into their food and folklore. In the seventeenth century, bunches of fresh basil were hung in doorways to protect homes against evil spirits and to ward off unwanted pests, such as flies. Basil has long been a symbol of love and romance in Europe: In Italy, when a young man wears a sprig of basil while courting a woman, it is a sign of serious intentions.

Thought to be a mild sedative, basil has appeared in a variety of home cures. Basil leaves have been added to bath waters, made into soothing teas, and combined with natural oils to be rubbed onto sore muscles. During the 1800s, Europeans and Americans frequently simmered the fresh herb in liquids such as water, wine, alcohol, or juice, along with other herbs and spices, and used the potion as a remedy for headaches and stomach maladies.

Cookbooks brought to the New World by colonists in the mid-1700s may have contributed to the general popularity of basil in America, but records also show that American Indians had been using fresh basil for decades prior to the colonists' arrival. By the late 1700s, basil began to appear in advertisements in American newspapers, and by the early 1800s it was frequently called for as an important ingredient in many cookbooks.

Although basil is most often associated with Italian food—especially with the wildly popular Italian pesto sauce—the herb is actually used throughout the entire Mediterranean, in parts of the Middle East, and particularly in Southeast Asia, where several varieties of basil often appear within a single dish. Frequently referred to as the "tomato herb," because its taste and vivid green color complement juicy red tomatoes so beautifully, basil also pairs well with all fruits and vegetables typical of the Mediterranean, as well as those of the tropics. It is particularly tasty when used with eggplant, summer squashes, onions, garlic, poultry, and mild-flavored fish and seafood. Asian cooks are fond of combining fresh basil with ingredients such as coconut milk, lime juice, fish sauce, beef, pork, shellfish, nuts and seeds, and noodles. But don't reserve this herb only for savory dishes; the sweet-spicy flavor of basil works well in many desserts, particularly ones that incorporate the fresh fruits of summer.

Fresh and dried basil are worlds apart in flavor, and most serious cooks use the dried version only when combined with other dried herbs, such as sage, oregano, thyme, and marjoram to form a dried herb "backbone" for long-cooking soups and stews. Dried basil is a poor substitute, at best, for the aromatic, leafy greens of fresh basil and is not used in recipes of this book because it bears little resemblance to the fresh herb.

Many recipes in this book call for a specific type of fresh basil, such as cinnamon basil or lemon basil. If these are not available, you may substitute the more prevalent fresh sweet basil. Although it is interesting to try the other, more unusual types of basil and the subtle nuances of each variety are pleasing, they are not crucial to the success of any given recipe in this book.

Basil begs to be eaten fresh from the garden. I recommend planting four or five different varieties because each flavor is distinct and delicious and all can be used in myriad ways. The plants grow favorably in well-drained, sunny spots in the garden and enjoy soil that is fairly fertile. For those who aren't inclined to grow it themselves, fresh basil is fortunately now available in most grocery stores, even during the winter months. Fresh basil will add sparkle and a touch of summer to your cooking, and it provides the inspiration for this collection of recipes.

A Compendium of Basil

Basil is an annual herb that grows in the warm spring and summer months and is always available fresh during those seasons. Small bunches of domestically grown fresh basil are usually available in grocery stores beginning around May, and larger, bushier, and less expensive bunches are abundant in stores during the hot summer months of June, July, August, and September. Fresh basil is cultivated somewhere in the world at all times, and is also grown in hothouses, so it is available during our cooler fall and winter seasons as well.

There are nearly sixty varieties of basil, and the most commonly available types include cinnamon basil, lemon basil, Thai basil, dark opal basil, and the ubiquitous sweet basil. In the San Francisco Bay Area, where I live, we are fortunate to have many excellent produce markets that offer a wide assortment of fresh herbs. The summer that I wrote this book I was able to find five different varieties of fresh basil. But even in areas without such extensive retail distribution of fresh herbs you can still find one or two of the more popular varieties of basil, such as sweet basil and dark opal basil, during summer months. If you live in a temperate climate or have access to specialty produce markets or gourmet grocery stores, you will be able to find fresh basil year-round. If you have difficulty locating some of the more exotic varieties of basil, the best way to ensure a high-quality, steady supply is to grow your own.

When purchasing any variety of fresh basil, look for healthy, unbruised, fresh leaves that are free of blemishes, and wholesome, firm stems. Flowering basil, rarely sold on the retail market, can have a more assertive flavor than basil that is still producing leaves. Both the flowers and the leaves are edible. The flowers can be used for garnishing savory or sweet dishes and are delicious added to salads.

Here are brief descriptions of some popular types of basil used for cooking:

Thai basil, also known as anise basil, has slightly serrated, purple-tinged green leaves that range in size from 1 to 1½ inches long and ½ to 1 inch wide. This large plant has white flowers that sport the same strong licorice flavor and aroma found in its leaves. With its bright citrus, mint, and grassy flavors, Thai basil is particularly good for use in baking, for flavoring vinegars and oils, and for seasoning Thai and Southeast Asian dishes.

Cinnamon basil is a very decorative plant with shiny foliage, lavender-white flowers, and bright green leaves that range in size from 1 to 1½ inches long and ½ to ¾ inch wide. Flowery, spicy, pungent, and almost juicy, these leaves have a distinct cinnamon flavor and are ideal for use in baking and for flavoring Mediterranean and Middle Eastern-style dishes.

Lemon basil is one of the smallest varieties of basil and has delicate leaves under 1 inch in length and ½ inch in width. Its relatively dull green leaves have a very assertive citrus scent and can almost be biting in flavor when raw. Their lemon taste is straightforward, pungent, strong, and ideal for pairing with fish, seafood, and poultry.

Dark opal basil, commonly used in Southeast Asian dishes, is one of the few basil varieties that have dark, shiny, purple leaves. Spiked around the edges, these 1-inch-long and ¾-inch-wide leaves have a deep, dusky flavor and aroma that are more complex than those of other types of basil. Because of its dark color, opal basil is not suitable for using in pesto, sauces, or in dishes cooked for long periods of time. Its beautiful appearance, however, makes it ideal for use in salads or stir-fries or as a garnish.

Sweet basil is the most widely grown basil and the most popular for use in cooking. Sweet basil is the variety used by herb and spice manufacturers in making dried basil. Its bright green, shiny, oval-shaped leaves can be 1½ to 2½ inches long and ½ to 1 inch wide. The leaves have the characteristic licorice flavor found in all basils, but they have strong herbal qualities as well. Their intense flavor affects the back of the tongue and exudes a very pleasing, pungent aftertaste. The taste of sweet basil can be longer-lasting yet one-dimensional in flavor in comparison with the other varieties. Sweet basil is most often used in classic Italian dishes, including the popular basil sauce called pesto; for garnishing pizza and *crostini;* and for pairing with fresh tomatoes in summer salads and entrées.

STORING BASIL

Always store fresh basil in the refrigerator. Basil is a delicate herb that tastes best if used within two days after purchasing, but it can last up to one week if very fresh when purchased and if properly stored. I prefer to keep basil wrapped in a plastic bag in the refrigerator. Some prefer storing it upright in a glass of water—much like a bouquet of flowers. I find that with this method the leaves wilt quickly and the stems can become soft and soggy. Another storage method is to remove the leaves from the stems, wash in cold water, and dry on paper towels. Place the washed leaves between two layers of paper towels, roll up, place in a plastic bag, and store in the refrigerator. This method is particularly helpful when the stems begin to soften and the leaves have started to turn brown and wilt.

For even longer storage, pack the leaves in olive oil and store in the refrigerator for up to one month. These leaves can be used in soups and stews, for pizza toppings, and in sauces and olive oil-based vinaigrettes. Basil leaves packed in olive oil aren't suitable for use in salads, because the leaves are too soggy, or in Asian dishes, because the flavor of the oil isn't compatible with Asian foods.

Freezing basil is the least successful method of storage because it leeches some of the vital oils from the leaves and turns them an unpleasant brown color. If you want to freeze basil for later use in cooking, I recommend pureeing the basil with garlic and enough oil to form a pestolike paste and storing the mixture in airtight containers in the freezer. You won't have the flexibility of using whole leaves, but the thawed mixture can be used in soups, sauces, stews, and dips; for sandwich spreads and pizza toppings; and, of course, for tossing with hot, cooked pasta.

PREPARING BASIL

To wash basil: Ideally, basil can be plucked from your garden and used unwashed. If you purchase your basil from a market, you may want to rinse it before using it for cooking. If the leaves show just a trace of dirt, rinse them under cold running water. If the leaves are particularly dirty, fill a large bowl with cold water, remove the leaves, and swish them around in the water. Remove the leaves from the water—do not drain the water and basil together as the dirt will adhere to the clean leaves! Depending on the recipe, you can dry the leaves in layers of paper towels, in a lettuce spinner, or use slightly damp. When adding basil to cooked foods, such as soups or stews, it's acceptable to use the leaves slightly damp, but if you will be finely chopping the basil, adding it to stir-fries or salads, or using it as a garnish, it's better to dry the leaves thoroughly.

To chiffonade basil: Take five or six large leaves of basil at a time and stack them together. Starting at the tips of the leaves, roll the stack into a thin tube. Using a very sharp chef's knife, slice across the width of the tube, making cuts ¼ inch (or smaller) apart. The resulting narrow strips of basil are called *chiffonade*. Basil chiffonade can be used in salads, added to hot soups just before serving, or used as a garnish.

To chop basil: Remove the leaves from the stems and place on a cutting board. Using a sharp chef's knife, begin cutting the leaves until the desired size is achieved. Coarsely chopped basil pieces are ¾ to 1 inch in size, medium chopped basil is about ½ inch in size, and finely chopped is smaller still.

To mince basil: Remove the leaves from the stems and place on a cutting board. Using a very sharp chef's knife, begin by coarsely chopping the leaves. Once the leaves are evenly chopped, continue chopping until the pieces of leaves are under ¼ inch in size. Be sure to use a very sharp knife; a dull knife will bruise the leaves, causing them to turn brown and soggy.

To puree basil: Basil leaves cannot be ground to a paste in a blender or food processor without some kind of liquid medium. The liquid used varies among recipes; oil, water, wine, or any appropriate spirit or vinegar can be used for this purpose. Pesto-making is a good example of this process because it combines oil and basil leaves, and occasionally a bit of water, to facilitate easy blending of all the ingredients.

COOKING BASIL

As with all fresh herbs, and in contrast to its dried counterpart, fresh basil must be added to hot food at the last minute or used as a garnish. Cooking fresh basil robs its leaves of their flavor and bright green color. Fresh basil cooked for longer than a few minutes eventually will become dark, marring the appearance of the finished dish. The finer the cut of basil, the faster it will assimilate into the flavors of hot dishes. For this reason, add finely minced basil later in the cooking process than you would coarsely chopped or whole basil leaves.

Appetizers

Crostini *with Tomato, Basil, and Greek Cheese*

*Greek manouri, a velvety and sumptuous sheep's milk cheese,
has the perfect texture and flavor for this simple appetizer. If you cannot find manouri,
you may use a mild goat or feta cheese. Since French feta is often more subtle in flavor and less
salty than Bulgarian or Greek feta, it is a good substitute for the soft, mild manouri.*

MAKES ABOUT 4 SERVINGS.

1 loaf (about 1 pound) French or Italian
   bread, cut into 12, ¾-inch-thick rounds
1 cup olive oil
5 cloves garlic, minced
1½ cups minced fresh sweet basil leaves

¾ pound manouri cheese, sliced into
   12 pieces
5 tomatoes, sliced into 12,
   ½-inch-thick rounds

Sprigs of basil, for garnish

Preheat oven to 400° F.

Arrange the bread slices in a single layer on baking sheets. Combine ½ cup of the olive oil with the garlic. Brush the tops of each bread slice with the oil-garlic mixture. Bake for 7 to 8 minutes or just until the surface turns light golden brown.

Remove from the oven.

In a small bowl, combine the remaining ½ cup olive oil and the minced basil; mix well.

Place 1 slice of cheese on each warm crouton (if using a soft cheese, spread the cheese onto the crouton). For each crouton, cover the cheese with about 1 teaspoon of the oil-basil mixture and top with a slice of tomato. Serve at room temperature, garnished with the sprigs of basil.

Cinnamon Basil and Feta Cheese-Stuffed New Potatoes

These bite-sized hors d'oeuvres, made with Greek olives,
cheese, and herbs typical of the Mediterranean, are excellent finger-food.
Served on a bed of mild and bitter greens, they also make an excellent lunch or light supper.
MAKES 4 TO 6 SERVINGS.

10 medium new potatoes (about 2 pounds)
Olive oil, for rubbing
¼ pound cream cheese, softened
⅓ pound feta cheese, crumbled
1 teaspoon minced fresh rosemary
1 cup minced fresh cinnamon basil or
    sweet basil leaves

1 tablespoon red wine vinegar
⅓ cup finely chopped pitted
    Kalamata olives
Salt and pepper, to taste

Sprigs of basil, for garnish

Preheat oven to 400° F.

Gently scrub the potatoes with a vegetable brush, removing any bits of dirt or mud. Pat dry and rub with the olive oil. Place in a single layer in a baking dish and bake for 45 minutes or until the potatoes are tender when pierced with a fork. Remove from the oven and cool to room temperature.

Cut each potato in half. Using a small spoon, gently scoop the pulp from each half into a medium bowl, leaving shells about ⅛ inch thick. Reserve the shells and mash the pulp with a fork.

To the potato pulp add the cream cheese, feta cheese, rosemary, minced basil, and red wine vinegar; mix well. Add the olives and mix just enough to incorporate into the potato mixture (overmixing will discolor the potatoes). Season with salt and pepper.

Fill each potato shell with some of the potato mixture. Serve at room temperature, garnished with the sprigs of basil.

Cinnamon Basil and Goat Cheese Spread

Simple and easy to prepare, this creamy spread is best when made one day ahead so that the flavors have time to "marry." Serve as a spread for crackers or rustic bread, stuffed into celery hearts, or spread onto cucumber rounds.

MAKES ABOUT 6 SERVINGS.

½ pound natural cream cheese
(free of stabilizers and gums)
¾ pound creamy goat cheese
2 cloves garlic, minced
1 teaspoon dried red pepper flakes

1½ cups minced fresh cinnamon basil
or sweet basil leaves
½ cup finely chopped toasted pistachio nuts
Salt and pepper, to taste

Sprigs of basil, for garnish

In a large bowl, combine the cream cheese, goat cheese, garlic, and red pepper flakes; mix well. Just before serving, add the minced basil and pistachios and mix well. Season with salt and pepper. Serve at room temperature, garnished with sprigs of basil.

To make basil-scented vodka: Combine 2 cups of minced basil leaves with 1 liter of vodka. Mix well and let stand, covered, in a nonreactive bottle for 2 weeks, shaking occasionally. Strain well and store vodka in a tightly sealed container. Use the vodka to make refreshing and unique spring or summer cocktails.

Pizzettas with Pesto and Assorted Toppings

*Pesto is a classic topping for pizza; when combined with
fresh vegetables and interesting cheeses or meats, the results are sensational. Serve these small
pizzas as an appetizer or with a salad for lunch or a light supper.*

MAKES 8 SMALL PIZZAS.

Pesto:

2 cups firmly packed fresh sweet basil leaves
3 cloves garlic
½ cup ground almonds
1 cup olive oil
Juice from 1 lemon
Salt and pepper, to taste

Pizza Dough:

1½ cups all-purpose flour
1½ cups bread flour
1 tablespoon kosher salt
1 package active dry yeast
(about 2¼ teaspoons)
1 cup warm water (110° to 115° F.)
6 tablespoons olive oil

Assorted Topping Combinations:

*Crumbled feta cheese, sliced, pitted
    Kalamata olives, and sliced fresh tomatoes*
*Sliced fresh mozzarella cheese and
    julienned sun-dried tomatoes*
Shelled prawns and sliced fresh fennel
Chopped smoked turkey and sliced red onion
*Sliced roasted red bell peppers and
    thinly sliced ham*
*Chopped cooked clams, sliced garlic,
    and chopped fresh parsley*
*Crumbled sausage, sliced red onions,
    and sliced fresh mozzarella cheese*
*Shredded smoked Cheddar and Monterey
    Jack cheeses and julienned red
    bell peppers*
*Sliced pitted green and oil-cured olives
    and crumbled goat cheese*
*Diced roasted new potatoes, crumbled
    Gorgonzola cheese, and toasted walnuts*
*Pine nuts, sliced garlic, and sliced
    fresh tomato*

To make the pesto: Place the basil, garlic, almonds, and olive oil in a blender or food processor. Blend until fairly smooth, scraping down the sides of the container from time to time. Add the lemon juice and mix well. Season with salt and pepper and transfer to a small nonreactive bowl (not copper or aluminum). Place a piece of plastic or parchment paper directly on the surface of the pesto to prevent it from browning. (The pesto can be made ahead and stored in the refrigerator for up to 1 week.)

To make the pizza dough: Place the flours and salt in a large bowl and mix well. In a small bowl, mix the yeast into the warm water, stirring until dissolved. Add the olive oil to the yeast mixture and mix well. Stirring with your hand, slowly add the liquid ingredients to the dry. Gather into a ball and turn out onto a lightly floured surface. If the dough is too wet, add a little more flour; if the dough is too dry, add a little more warm water.

Knead the dough for 4 or 5 minutes or until it is smooth and elastic; form into a ball. Transfer to a lightly greased bowl and cover with plastic wrap. Set in a warm place for 1½ to 2 hours to rise until doubled in size. (A gas oven with a pilot light is perfect for this.) Punch the dough down, remove from bowl, and knead on a lightly floured surface for 2 to 3 minutes; form into a ball. Cover with plastic wrap and let stand at room temperature for 40 to 45 minutes or until the dough does not spring back when poked with a finger.

To assemble and bake the pizzettas: Preheat two pizza stones in a 450° F. oven for 40 minutes. If you don't have pizza stones, use heavy baking sheets and preheat for 20 minutes. Meanwhile, divide the dough into 8 balls. Roll each ball out on a lightly floured surface, making even circles about ¼ inch thick. Place the dough on the hot stones and bake the dough blind (without toppings) for 5 minutes or until the crusts are light golden brown. Remove from the oven, spread with the pesto, and cover each with your choice of topping ingredients. Bake for 5 minutes or until the cheese (where applicable) just begins to melt and the toppings are hot. Remove from the oven, cut into quarters, and serve immediately.

Red Pepper Frittata with Basil

Served with roasted potatoes, interesting breads, and olives,
this colorful egg dish is ideal for breakfast or brunch, and when accompanied by
a green salad, it makes an excellent light lunch.

MAKES ABOUT 8 SERVINGS.

12 eggs, lightly beaten
½ cup milk
⅓ pound Parmesan cheese, grated
2 cups coarsely chopped fresh sweet
  basil leaves
2 teaspoons each salt and pepper

1 large onion, cut into small dice
¼ cup olive oil
1 red bell pepper, cut into small dice
2 teaspoons minced fresh thyme
1 teaspoon minced fresh oregano

Sprigs of basil, for garnish

Preheat oven to 350° F.

Combine the eggs, milk, Parmesan, chopped basil, and salt and pepper in a medium bowl. Set aside until needed.

In a 12-inch, nonstick, ovenproof sauté pan, sauté the onion in the olive oil over high heat for 5 minutes, stirring frequently. Add the red pepper, thyme, and oregano and cook for 3 to 4 minutes, stirring constantly. Add the egg mixture; reduce the heat to moderate and cook for 3 minutes, stirring constantly with a rubber spatula and scraping the bottom of the pan as if you were making scrambled eggs.

When the eggs are fairly firm, smooth the top with a spatula and place in the oven. Bake for 10 minutes or until the eggs are set all the way through to the center. Remove from the oven and cool to room temperature.

Invert the frittata onto a large plate and slice into wedges. Garnish with the sprigs of basil and serve.

Corn Crab Cakes with Lemon Basil Mayonnaise

*These crab cakes highlight the best flavors of summer and are terrific
served with a glass of champagne or crisp white wine. If you are pressed for time,
you can make the Lemon Basil Mayonnaise with commercial mayonnaise and simply add
the fresh basil and a clove of minced garlic.*

MAKES 6 TO 8 SERVINGS.

Lemon Basil Mayonnaise:

2 egg yolks
1 tablespoon Dijon mustard
½ cup olive oil
½ cup peanut oil
1 clove garlic, minced
*1 cup minced fresh lemon basil or
  sweet basil leaves*
2 teaspoons sherry vinegar
Salt and pepper, to taste

Corn Crab Cakes:

1 large onion, cut into small dice
1 tablespoon ground coriander seeds
3 tablespoons olive oil
2 tablespoons unsalted butter
2 cups fresh corn kernels
¼ cup sherry wine
½ pound crabmeat (about 2 cups)
2 eggs, lightly beaten
½ cup fine bread crumbs
1 cup mayonnaise
*1 cup coarsely chopped fresh
  sweet basil leaves*
Salt and pepper, to taste

Flour, for dredging
½ cup vegetable oil, for frying

To make the Lemon Basil Mayonnaise: Place the egg yolks and mustard in a small bowl
and whisk well. Slowly begin to add the olive oil a drop at a time, stirring constantly
with a wire whisk. When an emulsion starts to form and the mixture begins to thicken,

gradually add the remaining olive oil and the peanut oil in a thin stream, whisking constantly. Add the garlic, basil, and sherry vinegar and mix well. Season with salt and pepper. Cover and refrigerate until needed.

To make the Corn Crab Cakes: Sauté the onion and coriander in the olive oil and butter over moderate heat for 10 minutes, stirring occasionally. Add the corn and cook for 2 minutes. Add the sherry and cook for 5 minutes, stirring often. Remove from the heat, place in a large bowl, and cool to room temperature.

Add the crab, eggs, bread crumbs, mayonnaise, and basil; mix well and season with salt and pepper. Cover and refrigerate for at least 3 hours or up to 1 day.

To fry the crab cakes: Form the crab mixture into small patties using about 2 tablespoons for each cake. Dredge each pattie in just enough flour to coat all sides of the cake. Heat a thin layer of oil in a very large, nonstick sauté pan over moderately high heat. When the oil is moderately hot, add a small batch of cakes, allowing a ½-inch space between each cake. Fry the cakes on each side for 2 to 3 minutes until golden brown. Drain on paper towels. Cook the remaining cakes in batches, using more oil as needed. Serve hot, with the Lemon Basil Mayonnaise.

To ensure bushy, healthy basil plants, pinch the buds from the tops of the plants before they bloom. This encourages the plant to continue producing more leaves rather than flowers. If your plant does go to flower, snip them off and use as a garnish, or mince them and use in cooking.

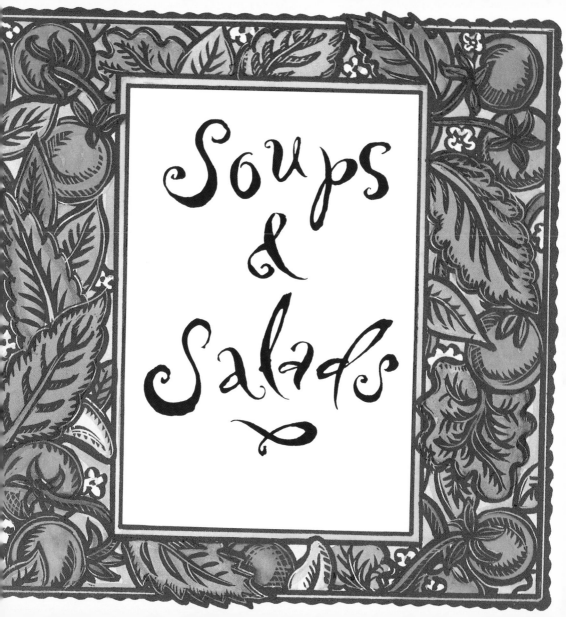

Soups
&
Salads

Corn Chowder with Tomatoes and Basil

*Rich, creamy, and irresistible, this summer soup is best
when served in small portions as a first course. Although this soup tastes
better if made with fresh corn, you can make this during other seasons with frozen corn.*

MAKES 6 SERVINGS.

1 large onion, cut into small dice
1 tablespoon ground coriander seeds
3 tablespoons olive oil
3 tablespoons unsalted butter
1 cup dry white wine
3 cups fresh corn kernels
6 cups light chicken stock or
   low-salt chicken broth

2 cups heavy cream
1 pint cherry tomatoes, stemmed
   and quartered
2 cups firmly packed fresh sweet basil
   leaves, cut into chiffonade
Salt and pepper, to taste

In a very large pot, sauté the onion and coriander in the olive oil and butter over moderate heat for 5 minutes, stirring frequently. Add the wine and cook until the liquid has evaporated, about 5 minutes.

Add the corn, chicken stock, and cream; bring to a boil over high heat and cook for 20 minutes, stirring frequently. Add the tomatoes and basil and cook for 2 minutes. Season with salt and pepper, and serve immediately.

Chilled English Pea Soup with Lemon Basil

*Fresh peas and mint are a classic combination and
when they are teamed with fresh lemon basil in this vivid green soup,
the result takes on a new dimension of flavor. This soup is perfect for lunch or dinner on a
hot summer day and would be delightful paired with a seafood salad.*

MAKES ABOUT 6 SERVINGS.

1 large onion, coarsely chopped
2 teaspoons ground anise seeds (see note)
1 teaspoon prepared curry powder
Pinch nutmeg
3 tablespoons olive oil
3 tablespoons unsalted butter
½ cup dry sherry wine
2 quarts light chicken stock or
   low-salt chicken broth

3 cups fresh English green peas
   (about 3 pounds, unshelled)
1 bunch green onions, green part only,
   coarsely chopped
1 cup coarsely chopped fresh mint leaves
2 cups coarsely chopped fresh lemon basil
   or sweet basil leaves
Salt and pepper, to taste

Basil leaves, for garnish

In a very large pot, sauté the onion and spices in the olive oil and butter over moderate heat for 10 minutes. Add the sherry and cook until the liquid has evaporated, about 5 minutes.

Add the chicken stock, peas, and green onions; bring to a boil over high heat. Reduce the heat to moderate and simmer for 20 minutes or until the peas are tender. Remove from heat, add the mint and chopped basil, and mix well; cool slightly.

In batches, puree the soup in a blender until smooth. Strain through a fine wire sieve or food mill into a large bowl. Season with salt and pepper. Cover and refrigerate for at least 6 hours or up to 2 days. Serve chilled, garnished with the basil leaves.

Note: Grind seeds in spice or coffee grinder or by hand, using a small mortar and pestle.

Cucumber and Lemon Basil Yogurt Soup

*The refreshing flavor of cucumber combined
with juicy, sweet honeydew melon makes a light, cooling, summer soup.
Although I prefer the texture and flavor of full-fat yogurt for this simple soup, low-fat or
nonfat yogurt would make this dish virtually fat free.*
MAKES 4 TO 6 SERVINGS.

2 large cucumbers, peeled, seeded,
   and coarsely chopped
2 cups coarsely chopped lemon basil or
   sweet basil leaves
1 cup coarsely chopped, peeled, and
   seeded honeydew melon

½ cup chopped fresh chives
1½ cups plain yogurt
Salt and pepper, to taste
1 cup loosely packed fresh lemon basil
   or sweet basil leaves, cut into chiffonade

Combine the cucumbers, chopped basil, honeydew melon, and chives in a large bowl; mix well. In batches, puree in a blender until smooth. Strain through a fine wire sieve or food mill into a large bowl. Add the yogurt and season with salt and pepper. Cover and refrigerate for at least 6 hours or up to 2 days. Serve chilled, garnished with the basil chiffonade.

The Complete American Housewife, *written in 1776,
suggests a formula of dried mint, cloves, and basil to "induce
sleep and fragrant dreams." This combination of dried herbs
was often used for tea or stuffed into pillows to aid the sleep-
ing and dreaming process.*

Thai Chicken and Eggplant Salad with Thai and Opal Basils

Aromatic and complex in flavor, texture, and color, this classic Thai dish
is wonderful served with basmati or jasmine rice or even plain steamed white or brown rice.
MAKES 4 SERVINGS.

Dressing:

⅓ cup peanut oil
3 tablespoons fish sauce (nuoc cham)
¼ cup lime juice
2 cloves garlic, thinly sliced
5 Serrano or jalapeño peppers, stemmed
 and sliced into thin rounds
1 cup minced fresh Thai basil leaves
Salt and pepper, to taste

Salad:

¼ cup peanut oil
2 Japanese eggplants (about ¾ pound),
 halved lengthwise and cut on the diagonal
 into 1-inch pieces
2 boneless, skinless chicken breast halves,
 cut into ½-inch strips
½ cup chicken stock
1 small red onion, thinly sliced
½ cup loosely packed fresh cilantro leaves
1 cup loosely packed fresh opal basil
 or sweet basil leaves
Salt and pepper, to taste
6 large red leaf lettuce leaves

To make the dressing: Place the peanut oil in a medium nonreactive bowl. Using a whisk, slowly add the fish sauce and lime juice, whisking constantly to form a smooth emulsion. Add the garlic, chili peppers, and basil; mix well and season with salt and pepper. Set aside until needed.

To make the salad: Heat the peanut oil in a large, nonstick sauté pan. When the oil is hot but not smoking, add the eggplant and cook over high heat for 3 to 4 minutes, stirring constantly. Add the chicken and chicken stock and cook for 5 minutes or until the eggplant is very tender and the chicken is cooked through.

Place the chicken and eggplant in a large bowl. Add the red onion, cilantro, opal basil, and the dressing; mix well. Season with salt and pepper. Arrange the lettuce leaves on a serving platter and top with the chicken-eggplant mixture. Serve warm or at room temperature.

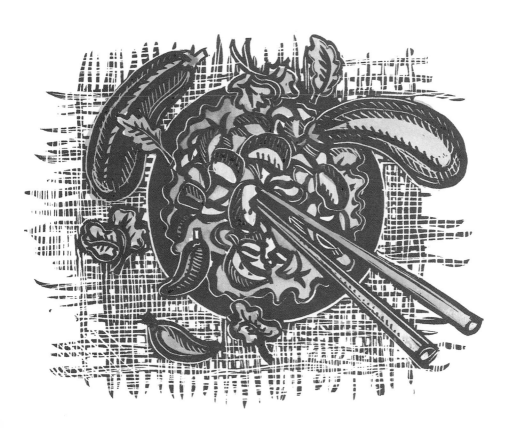

Grilled Prawn Salad with Cinnamon Basil and Feta Cheese

*If you prefer cooking indoors rather than grilling outdoors, for this
recipe you may roast the prawns in a baking dish, along with the marinade, in a
450° F. oven. Cook for 5 to 7 minutes or just until the prawns are opaque to the center.*

MAKES 4 SERVINGS.

¾ cup olive oil
2 cloves garlic, minced
1 tablespoon ground coriander seeds
1 cup minced fresh cinnamon basil or
   sweet basil leaves
1 pound large prawns, skins and
   tails removed

1 cup loosely packed arugula leaves
1½ cups coarsely chopped fresh
   cinnamon basil or sweet basil leaves
2 roasted red bell peppers, peeled, seeded,
   and thinly sliced (about ¾ cup)
½ pound feta cheese, crumbled
Freshly cracked black pepper

Combine ½ cup of the olive oil and the garlic, coriander seed, and minced basil in
a medium nonreactive bowl. Add the prawns, cover, and marinate at room temperature for 1 hour or in the refrigerator overnight.

    Prepare a charcoal grill. When the coals are medium-hot (a light layer of gray ash
covers the coals), place the prawns on the grill and cook, basting with the marinade
and rotating to cook evenly, for 4 to 5 minutes or just until they are opaque to the
center. Remove from the grill.

    Arrange the arugula and chopped basil on a large platter. Top with the warm
prawns, roasted peppers, and feta cheese. Drizzle with the remaining ¼ cup olive
oil and sprinkle with freshly cracked black pepper.

Spicy Vietnamese Mussel Salad with Thai Basil and Mint

*I prefer to use the large, plump, slightly sweet Greenlip mussels
imported from New Zealand for this seafood dish, but you can use any
fresh mussels that are available. For a slightly heartier salad, cooked diced chicken, beef,
or duck can be used in place of the mussels.*

MAKES 4 SERVINGS.

Dressing:

½ cup peanut oil
3 tablespoons fish sauce (nuoc cham)
3 tablespoons fresh lime juice
2 teaspoons sugar
1 clove garlic, minced
1 or 2 jalapeño peppers, stemmed, seeded,
   and finely chopped

Salad:

2 pounds medium to medium-large mussels
   (be sure to buy mussels with closed shells)
1½ cups dry white wine
1 cup coarsely chopped fresh sweet
   basil leaves
4 cups finely shredded savoy or
   white cabbage
1 carrot, shredded
1 cup firmly packed fresh Thai basil leaves
1 cup loosely packed fresh mint leaves

⅔ cup roasted peanuts, coarsely chopped,
   for garnish

To make the dressing: Place the peanut oil in a small bowl. Slowly add the fish sauce and lime juice, stirring constantly with a wire whisk. Add the sugar and stir until dissolved. Add the garlic and jalapeño peppers; mix well. Set aside until needed.

To make the salad: Scrub the mussels with a wire brush and remove the beards and any sand or grit. Place mussels in a large, shallow pan, along with the wine and chopped sweet basil. Bring to a boil over high heat. Reduce the heat to moderate, cover, and cook for 5 to 6 minutes or until most of the shells have opened. Remove all the mussels that have opened and place in a colander. Cook the remaining mussels for 2 additional minutes. Remove any opened mussels and add to the colander; discard any that have not opened.

When the mussels are cool enough to handle, remove the meat from the shells; set aside until needed and discard shells.

Place the cabbage, carrot, and the Thai basil and mint leaves in a large bowl. Add three-quarters of the dressing and mix well. Transfer to a large platter and top with the mussels. Drizzle with the remaining dressing, garnish with the peanuts, and serve immediately.

To make basil vinegar: Fill a wide-mouth jar with coarsely chopped basil leaves of any variety. Cover with white wine or champagne vinegar and let stand, covered, for at least three weeks. Strain, and store the vinegar in a tightly sealed jar or bottle for up to one year.

Poached Scallops with Deep-fried Basil

*Elegant and impressive, this delicate seafood dish
is best if made with large, fresh sea scallops rather than small bay
scallops. It is ideal for a light appetizer. You can prepare the vinaigrette and fry the
basil up to 4 or 5 hours prior to serving, leaving only the poaching to be done at the last minute.*
MAKES 4 SERVINGS.

¼ cup hazelnut oil
1 clove garlic, minced
1½ tablespoons raspberry vinegar
Salt and pepper, to taste
1 cup vegetable oil, for frying
2 cups loosely packed thoroughly dried
   fresh sweet basil leaves

1 cup dry white wine
½ pound sea scallops, small muscles removed
1 head radicchio, trimmed, tough outer
   leaves discarded, inner leaves separated
¼ cup toasted hazelnuts, coarsely chopped

To make the vinaigrette, place the hazelnut oil and garlic in a small bowl. Slowly add the vinegar, whisking constantly to form a smooth emulsion. Season with salt and pepper, and set aside until needed.

Place the oil in a deep-sided saucepan. Heat over high heat until the oil reaches a temperature of about 360° F. on a deep-frying thermometer. Add half of the basil and fry for 45 seconds or until the leaves are crispy and dark green. Remove with a slotted spoon or strainer and drain on paper towels. Repeat with the remaining basil. In a shallow skillet, bring the wine to boil over high heat. Add the scallops, reduce the heat to moderately high, and cook for about 2 minutes, flipping each scallop after the first minute to promote even cooking. When scallops are almost opaque throughout, remove immediately with a slotted spoon and drain on paper towels.

In a small bowl, toss the radicchio with three-quarters of the vinaigrette. Arrange on a serving platter. Gently toss scallops and hazelnuts with the remaining vinaigrette; mix well. Arrange scallop mixture over the radicchio. Garnish with the deep-fried basil and serve immediately.

Angel Hair Pasta with Lemon Basil, Asparagus, and Scallops

Served hot or at room temperature, this colorful pasta dish highlights
the best of summer produce. Pair with mixed greens and Italian bread for a delightful dinner.
MAKES 4 TO 6 SERVINGS.

½ cup plus 2 tablespoons extra-virgin
   olive oil
1 pound bay scallops, small muscles removed
1 tablespoon fennel seeds
4 large tomatoes, cut into small dice
4 cloves garlic, minced
3 cups finely chopped fresh lemon basil
   or sweet basil leaves

1 pound angel hair pasta
1 pound thin asparagus, trimmed and cut
   into 1-inch pieces
3 tablespoons sherry vinegar
Salt and pepper, to taste

1 cup toasted pine nuts, for garnish

Heat 2 tablespoons of the olive oil in a large, nonstick sauté pan over high heat until the oil is hot but not smoking. Add the scallops and fennel seeds and cook over high heat for 2 to 3 minutes, stirring constantly, until the scallops are almost opaque throughout. Remove from the pan and place in a large serving bowl.

To the scallops add the tomatoes, garlic, and basil; mix well.

Meanwhile, cook the pasta in a large pot of salted boiling water for 4 minutes. Add the asparagus and cook for 45 seconds. Drain well and add to the scallop-vegetable mixture; mix well. Add the remaining ½ cup olive oil, and the sherry vinegar, salt, and pepper; mix well. Garnish with the pine nuts, and serve immediately.

Linguine with Basil, Walnuts, and Gorgonzola

Serve this rich and filling pasta dish with a salad of mild and bitter greens, slices of toasted bread, and glasses of red wine for a memorable cool-weather dinner. Imported Italian Gorgonzola cheese is sweeter and can be milder than other imported and domestic blue cheeses, but if the Italian blue isn't available you may substitute any double or triple crème, soft-ripened mild blue cheese such as Blue Castello, Pipo Crème, Danablu, or Camembleu.

MAKES 4 TO 6 SERVINGS.

1 large onion, thinly sliced
6 cloves garlic, minced
1 tablespoon minced fresh rosemary
¼ cup olive oil
1½ cups toasted walnuts, coarsely chopped
¾ pound linguine
¾ pound imported Gorgonzola cheese, crumbled

¼ cup balsamic vinegar
2½ cups coarsely chopped fresh sweet basil leaves
Salt and pepper, to taste

In a large sauté pan, sauté the onion, garlic, and rosemary in the olive oil over moderate heat for 10 minutes, stirring occasionally. Remove from the heat and place in a very large serving bowl. Add the walnuts, mix well, and set aside until needed.

Meanwhile, cook the linguine in salted boiling water for 8 to 10 minutes or until *al dente*. Drain well and add to the onion mixture. Add the cheese and balsamic vinegar and mix well. Add the basil, salt, and pepper and mix well. Serve immediately.

To grow enough basil to make six pints of pesto sauce, plant at least three small pots of sweet basil.

Burmese Coconut Chicken with Thai and Opal Basils

*Luscious and spicy, serve this simple Burmese curry with steamed rice
and stir-fried vegetables to make a complete meal. Coconut milk can be found in Asian,
Latin, and natural food stores, gourmet food shops, and some grocery stores.*

MAKES 4 SERVINGS.

2 tablespoons peanut oil
4 chicken thighs
4 chicken legs
2 large onions, cut into ½-inch wedges
4 cloves garlic, thinly sliced
3 jalapeño peppers, stemmed and
   thinly sliced
1 tablespoon ground caraway seeds (see note)
1 teaspoon ground cinnamon

2 cans (14 ounces each) coconut milk
   (about 3½ cups)
2 cups coarsely chopped fresh Thai basil
   or sweet basil leaves
2 cups coarsely chopped fresh opal basil
   leaves
Salt and pepper, to taste

Preheat oven to 400° F.

In a large, nonstick skillet, heat the peanut oil over moderate heat. Add the chicken in batches and brown on all sides. Remove with a slotted spoon and place in a baking dish large enough to accommodate the chicken and the coconut milk in one layer.

Using the same skillet, and the oil and chicken fat remaining in it, cook the onions, garlic, jalapeño peppers, caraway, and cinnamon over high heat for 5 minutes, stirring constantly. Remove from the heat and add to the chicken. Pour the coconut milk into the hot skillet and stir, scraping the bottom to remove any browned particles. Add to the onions and chicken and mix well.

Bake, uncovered, for 1½ hours. Remove from the oven, add the basil, and mix gently. Season with salt and pepper, and serve immediately.

Note: Grind seeds in spice or coffee grinder or by hand, using a small mortar and pestle.

Roast Cornish Game Hens Stuffed with Two Basils

These small birds are delicious paired with the subtle flavors of orange zest and two types of fresh basil. Accompany the Cornish game hens with vegetables and wild rice or roast potatoes for a satisfying dinner. This recipe can serve two people one game hen each; for lighter appetites it can serve four people half a game hen each. If you are preparing it for four people with substantial appetites, double the recipe.

MAKES 2 TO 4 SERVINGS.

1 cup coarsely chopped fresh
    opal basil leaves
1 cup coarsely chopped fresh
    sweet basil leaves
Zest and juice from 1 orange
2 Cornish game hens, patted dry
Olive oil, for rubbing
Black pepper

Preheat oven to 425° F.

In a bowl, combine the basils, orange zest, and orange juice; mix well. Tightly pack the basil mixture inside the cavity of each hen. Tie the legs together with kitchen twine and tuck the wings under. Rub the hens with olive oil and sprinkle with black pepper. Place, breast sides up, on a roasting rack set inside a lightly greased roasting pan.

Roast for 10 minutes. Remove from the oven and rotate the hens so that the breasts face down. Roast for 30 minutes longer. To check for doneness, prick the underside of the thighs with a sharp fork; if the juices run clear, the hens are done. Remove from the oven and let stand at room temperature for 5 minutes before serving.

Stir-fried Duck Breast with Cinnamon Basil and Ginger

*This colorful stir-fry draws from both Chinese and Southeast Asian
ingredients and is ideal for a light lunch if served with steamed basmati rice or cooked noodles.*

MAKES 4 SERVINGS.

3 tablespoons peanut oil
2 boneless, skinless duck breast halves,
   sliced into ½-inch strips
1 small red bell pepper, cut into julienne
3 cloves garlic, minced
4-inch piece gingerroot, peeled
   and slivered

3 tablespoons sherry wine
2 tablespoons soy sauce
1½ cups coarsely chopped fresh
   cinnamon basil or sweet basil leaves

Sprigs of basil, for garnish

Heat the peanut oil in a large, nonstick sauté pan or wok over high heat. When the oil is hot but not smoking add the duck and red pepper and cook, stirring constantly, for 2 minutes. Add the garlic and ginger and cook 1 minute. Add the sherry, soy sauce, and chopped basil and cook for 1 minute, stirring constantly. Remove from the heat and serve immediately, garnished with the sprigs of basil.

Like recipes for many traditional dishes, formulas for pesto are countless and varied. In Genoa, Italy, where pesto was invented, different versions incorporate a wide variety of ingredients, including spinach, parsley, cream, butter, walnuts, almonds, pistachio nuts—even pancetta. There really isn't one correct recipe for pesto sauce—it's up to the individual cook to create a recipe to suit a particular dish.

Roast Salmon with Corn and Lemon Basil Salad

Tender, young white corn, straight from the farm, requires no cooking; simply shave the kernels from the cob and use raw. If you are using more mature white or yellow corn, follow the directions for cooking it in the beginning of the recipe. You can find seasoned rice wine vinegar in Asian markets and most grocery stores.

MAKES 4 SERVINGS.

3 cups corn kernels (about 4 medium ears)
2 large tomatoes, cored and cut
   into small dice
1 cup finely chopped fresh lemon basil
   or sweet basil leaves
⅓ cup plus 3 tablespoons olive oil

2 tablespoons seasoned rice wine vinegar
Salt and pepper, to taste
4 fresh salmon fillets or steaks
   (6 to 8 ounces each)

Sprigs of basil, for garnish

Preheat oven to 450° F.

Cook the corn kernels in a pot of salted boiling water for 2 minutes; drain well and dry on paper towels. (If using tender, young white corn kernels eliminate this step.)

Place the corn, tomatoes, basil, ⅓ cup of the olive oil, and the vinegar in a large bowl; mix well. Season with salt and pepper and transfer to a large, shallow serving platter.

Rub the salmon on all sides with the remaining 3 tablespoons of olive oil. Place in a baking dish and roast for 6 or 7 minutes or just until small white spots appear on the surface of the fish and the center is opaque throughout. Remove from the oven and arrange on top of the corn-tomato mixture. Serve immediately, garnished with the sprigs of basil.

Pan-fried Pork Tenderloin with
Fennel, Sun-dried Tomatoes, and Basil

*Tender rounds of lean pork tenderloin are the perfect foil for the harmonious flavors of
fresh fennel, basil, and dried tomatoes. I like to buy sun-dried tomatoes in bulk rather than
packed in oil. They are less expensive this way and can be easily reconstituted in hot water—
eliminating the excess calories of the oil-packed variety. To reconstitute sun-dried tomatoes,
place in a bowl and cover with very hot water until tender, 30 minutes to 1 hour depending on
how fresh or dry the tomatoes are. Drain them well before using them in this recipe.*

MAKES 4 TO 6 SERVINGS.

¼ cup plus 3 tablespoons olive oil
2-pound pork tenderloin, sliced into
   ¾-inch thick rounds
1 medium onion, halved and cut into
   medium wedges
3 bulbs fennel, trimmed, tough outer
   leaves discarded, sliced into medium
   wedges

2 teaspoons fennel seeds
1 teaspoon minced dried rosemary
¾ cup finely chopped reconstituted
   sun-dried tomatoes
½ cup Madeira or sherry wine
2 cups loosely packed fresh sweet basil leaves
Salt and pepper, to taste

In a large sauté pan, heat 3 tablespoons of the olive oil over moderate heat. Add the
pork and cook over high heat for 3 to 4 minutes per side or until golden brown and the
insides are just barely pink. Remove from the pan, cover, and keep warm in a low oven
while you cook the remaining ingredients.

    In the same pan, heat the remaining ¼ cup olive oil over high heat. Add the onion,
fennel, fennel seeds, rosemary, and sun-dried tomatoes. Cook over high heat for
5 minutes, stirring constantly. Add the Madeira and cook for 1 minute. Add the basil
and cook for 30 seconds or until it just starts to wilt. Season with salt and pepper; mix
well. Remove from the pan and transfer to a serving platter or to individual plates. Top
with the pork, and serve immediately.

Baked Whole Snapper Stuffed with Cinnamon Basil and Onions

Redolent with basil, this lean fish entrée takes only minutes of preparation before baking and is easy to serve. Crusty bread or rice would be a good accompaniment for the tender snapper.

MAKES 4 TO 6 SERVINGS.

1 large onion, halved and cut
 into ½-inch wedges
3 cloves garlic, thinly sliced
¼ cup olive oil
1 tablespoon minced fresh oregano

4 cups loosely packed fresh cinnamon basil
 or sweet basil leaves
Salt and pepper, to taste
4-pound whole red snapper, cleaned,
 with head on
1 lemon, thinly sliced

Preheat oven to 425° F.

In a very large sauté pan, cook the onion and garlic in the olive oil over high heat for 5 minutes, stirring frequently. Add the oregano and basil and cook for 30 seconds. Season with salt and pepper.

Stuff the inside of the snapper with the onion-basil mixture. Place the lemon slices on top of the stuffing and press firmly to secure the ingredients inside the fish. Place in a lightly greased roasting pan and bake uncovered for 10 minutes.

Remove from the oven and cover with foil. Bake for an additional 25 to 30 minutes or just until the fish is opaque in the center and tender throughout. Cut fish into individual portions, and serve along with the onion-basil stuffing.

Spiced Potato and Basil Gratin

Don't be deceived by the word "spiced" in the title of this recipe. This rich gratin is spiked with aromatic, sweet-savory spices—not the fiery variety. A wedge of this gratin presented on a bed of bitter greens and paired with a glass of dry white wine would make a fine lunch.

MAKES 6 SERVINGS.

6 medium boiling potatoes
2 cups loosely packed fresh sweet basil leaves
2½ cups heavy cream
1 tablespoon ground coriander seeds

1 teaspoon each *salt, black pepper, mace, and allspice*
¼ pound fontina or domestic provolone cheese, grated

Preheat oven to 375° F.

Cook the potatoes in a pot of salted boiling water for 10 minutes. Drain and cool to room temperature. When cool enough to handle, remove the skins and cut the potatoes into ¼-inch slices.

Arrange one-third of the potato slices in a thin layer on the bottom of a round, 10-inch baking dish rubbed lightly with olive oil. Sprinkle one-third of the basil over the potatoes. Cover with half of the remaining potatoes, and the remaining basil. Finally, top with the remaining potatoes.

Combine the cream and spices in a small bowl. Slowly drizzle the mixture over the potatoes. Bake for 1½ hours or until the cream is thick and the potatoes are very tender. Sprinkle the cheese over the top; bake for 5 minutes longer or until the cheese is melted. Remove from the oven and let stand at room temperature for 10 minutes before serving.

Thai Beef Curry with Anise and Two Basils

This spicy, herbaceous Thai dish is excellent served hot, with basmati rice, but also makes a wonderful lunch served cold, on a bed of shredded cabbage. Look for many of the ingredients in Asian markets. You may increase the amount of jalapeño peppers if you prefer very spicy food. To facilitate slicing the beef, place the meat in the freezer for one hour before slicing.

MAKES 4 TO 6 SERVINGS.

1 pound beef sirloin, cut into
   paper-thin slices
¼ cup fresh lime juice
3 tablespoons fish sauce (nuoc cham)
1 tablespoon ground star anise (see note)
2 tablespoons peanut oil
1 small onion, thinly sliced
4 red jalapeño peppers, stemmed and
   thinly sliced
4 cloves garlic, thinly sliced

1 teaspoon each ground fenugreek, fennel,
   caraway, and coriander seeds (see note)
1 cup coarsely chopped fresh Thai
   basil leaves
1 cup coarsely chopped fresh opal basil
   or sweet basil leaves
Salt and pepper, to taste

¾ cup coarsely chopped toasted
   peanuts, for garnish

In a nonreactive dish, marinate the beef in the lime juice, fish sauce, and anise for 30 minutes at room temperature.

In a large, nonstick sauté pan or wok, heat the peanut oil over high heat. When the oil just begins to smoke, add the onion, jalapeño peppers, garlic, spices, beef, and the marinade. Cook over high heat for 2 minutes, stirring constantly. Remove from the heat, add the basils, and mix well. Season with salt and pepper. Transfer to a serving platter and garnish with the peanuts. Serve immediately.

Note: Grind the spices in a spice or coffee grinder or by hand, using a small mortar and pestle.

Onion, Fennel, and Goat Cheese Tart with Basil

This flavorful tart is perfect for those who like to avoid eggs and cream but still like the idea of eating a savory pie filled with vegetables and cheese. If you aren't a big fan of goat cheese, you may substitute feta cheese.

MAKES 6 SERVINGS.

Crust:

2 cups all-purpose flour
1 tablespoon ground fennel seeds (see note)
2 teaspoons salt
6 tablespoons unsalted butter,
    cut into very small pieces
3 to 4 tablespoons ice water

Filling:

1 large onion, halved and cut into
    ¼-inch wedges
2 bulbs fennel, trimmed, tough outer
    leaves discarded, thinly sliced
¼ cup extra-virgin olive oil
2 teaspoons dried thyme
½ cup vermouth
2 cups coarsely chopped fresh
    sweet basil leaves
½ pound goat cheese, crumbled
Salt and pepper, to taste

To make the crust: Place the flour, fennel seeds, and salt in a medium bowl; mix well. Using your fingers, mix in the butter, one piece at a time, until the mixture resembles coarse meal. Add just enough ice water to form the mixture into a ball. Wrap in plastic and refrigerate for at least 1 hour or up to 2 days.

Preheat oven to 400° F.

Remove dough from refrigerator (if refrigerated for longer than 2 hours, remove dough 1 hour before using). On a lightly floured surface, roll the dough into a 14-inch circle. Gently fit the dough into a 12-inch tart pan, and form a ¼-inch edge up over the sides of the pan to allow for shrinkage while baking. Cover the bottom and sides of the dough with parchment paper or foil and fill with pie weights or dried beans. Bake for 15 minutes. Remove the pie weights and bake an additional 10 minutes or until the bottom and sides are light golden brown. Remove from the oven and cool to room temperature.

To make the filling: Cook the onion and fennel in the olive oil over high heat for 7 minutes or until slightly wilted, stirring frequently. Add the thyme and vermouth, reduce the heat to moderate, and cook until the liquid has evaporated, about 5 minutes. Remove from the heat and transfer to a bowl. Add the basil and mix well; cool to room temperature. When the mixture is cool, add the goat cheese and mix gently. Season with salt and pepper.

Fill the tart shell with the onion-fennel mixture and bake for 10 minutes or until the cheese is soft and hot. Remove from the oven. Cut into wedges and serve warm or at room temperature.

Note: Grind the fennel seeds in a spice or coffee grinder or by hand, using a small mortar and pestle.

Desserts

Poached Peaches with Cinnamon Basil Crème Fraîche

Make this delightful dessert in the height of summer,
when peaches are plump and juicy and basil is abundant. If you
cannot find crème fraîche you may substitute sour cream or full-fat plain yogurt.
To peel the peaches, drop into a large pot of boiling water for 30 seconds. Remove with
a slotted spoon and drain in a colander. When cool enough to handle, slip the skins off and discard.
MAKES 4 SERVINGS.

Peaches:

2 cups sparkling wine
2 cups water
1 cup loosely packed fresh cinnamon basil
*   or sweet basil leaves*
3 large freestone peaches, peeled, pitted,
*   and cut into eighths*

Cinnamon Basil Crème Fraîche:

1 cup crème fraîche
1½ tablespoons almond liqueur
½ cup minced fresh cinnamon basil
*   or sweet basil leaves*
Pinch of nutmeg

Sprigs of basil, for garnish

To make the peaches: Place the sparkling wine, water, and basil in a deep saucepan. Bring to a boil over high heat and cook for 5 minutes. Add the peaches and return to a boil. Reduce the heat to moderate and cook for 3 or 4 minutes or until the fruit is tender, but not mushy. Using a slotted spoon, carefully remove the peaches from the liquid and divide among four shallow serving bowls. Cool to room temperature or chill. Strain the poaching liquid and set aside until needed.

To make the Cinnamon Basil Crème Fraîche: In a small bowl, combine the crème fraîche, almond liqueur, minced basil, and nutmeg; mix well.

To serve the peaches, add some of the poaching liquid to each bowl of peaches. Drizzle each with Cinnamon Basil Crème Fraîche and garnish with the sprigs of basil.

Spiced Pound Cake with Lemon Basil-Orange Syrup

*Dense and moist, this lightly spiced pound cake makes a lovely warm-weather dessert;
the Lemon Basil-Orange syrup is the perfect flavor companion for this buttery cake.
This recipe makes two loaf cakes; if you can only use one at a time I suggest freezing the second
cake, wrapped tightly in plastic and then in foil. However, once the cakes are drizzled with
the syrup they will keep at cool room temperature for up to one week.*

MAKES ABOUT 20 SERVINGS (2 LOAF CAKES).

Cake:

¾ pound (3 sticks) unsalted butter,
  at room temperature
1 pound powdered sugar
6 large eggs, lightly beaten
1 tablespoon vanilla extract
2¾ cups sifted all-purpose flour
1 tablespoon nutmeg

Lemon Basil-Orange Syrup:

1 cup orange juice
½ cup water
2 cups sugar
1 cup minced fresh lemon basil or
  sweet basil leaves

Sprigs of basil, for garnish

To make the cake: Preheat oven to 300° F. Grease two 9-by-5-inch loaf pans and dust
lightly with flour.

In a large bowl, beat the butter with an electric mixer until creamy. Gradually sift
the powdered sugar into the butter, stirring occasionally to partially combine. When
all the sugar has been added, beat until fluffy. Gradually add the eggs, beating well
after each addition. Add the vanilla, flour, and nutmeg; mix well. Divide the batter
between the two pans.

Bake on the bottom rack of oven for 45 minutes. Rotate the pans to the top rack
and bake for 10 minutes longer or until a toothpick inserted into the centers of the
cakes comes out clean.

Remove from the oven and cool in pans for 30 minutes.

Meanwhile, make the Lemon Basil-Orange Syrup: Place the orange juice, water, sugar, and basil in a deep-sided saucepan. Bring to a boil over high heat and cook for 15 minutes, stirring frequently to prevent the mixture from boiling over. When the mixture is thick and syrupy, remove from the heat and strain. Cool to room temperature. If the syrup becomes thicker than pouring consistency, thin with about 2 tablespoons of very hot water.

Using a long, thin, wooden skewer, poke each cake all over from the top to the bottom. Drizzle half of the syrup over each cake, taking care to spread the syrup evenly into the tiny holes. Let cakes stand at least 2 hours before serving or cover with foil and keep up to 1 week in the pan. To serve, remove the room-temperature cakes from pans and cut into 1-inch slices. Garnish with the sprigs of basil.

Summer Berries and Figs with Honey-Basil Cream

The spicy flavor of basil paired with fresh figs and summer berries in this unique dessert is sure to leave a lasting impression on you and your dining companions. If you cannot find the summer fruits specified in this recipe, substitute any assortment of seasonal fresh fruits.
Serve with dessert wine or champagne.

MAKES 4 TO 6 SERVINGS.

Honey-Basil Cream:
1 pint heavy cream
½ cup water
2 tablespoons honey
1 cup finely chopped fresh sweet
    basil leaves
1 teaspoon vanilla extract

Figs and Berries:
1 pint Black Mission figs, trimmed
    and halved (quartered if large)
½ pint strawberries, stemmed and
    halved
½ pint raspberries
½ pint blackberries

Sprigs of basil, for garnish

To make the Honey-Basil Cream: Place the cream, water, and honey in a large, heavy-bottomed saucepan. Bring to a boil over high heat, stirring frequently to prevent the mixture from boiling over. Add the basil and reduce the heat to moderate; cook for 20 minutes or until the cream is thick and pale brown. Add the vanilla and mix well. Strain through a fine wire sieve and transfer to a small saucepan. Keep warm over low heat until ready to use.

Combine the figs and berries in a large bowl; mix gently. Arrange in serving dishes and drizzle with the warm Honey-Basil Cream. Garnish with the sprigs of basil, and serve immediately.

Chocolate-Hazelnut Torte with Cinnamon Basil

Rich, moist, and laced with basil, this hazelnut torte
needs no icing or frosting—a simple dollop of whipped cream, crème fraîche,
or vanilla ice cream would be sensational. Serve the torte warm or at room temperature.
MAKES 12 SERVINGS (TWO 8-INCH CAKES).

8 ounces semisweet chocolate
6 ounces (1½ sticks) unsalted butter
1 cup minced fresh cinnamon basil or
   sweet basil leaves
4 eggs, separated
¾ cup sugar
1 cup finely chopped toasted hazelnuts
2 tablespoons sifted all-purpose flour

Whipped cream, for garnish
Sprigs of basil, for garnish

Preheat oven to 350° F. Grease two 8-inch cake pans and dust lightly with flour.

In the top of a double boiler, melt the chocolate and butter over barely simmering water, stirring until melted and smooth. Remove the top of the boiler from heat and add the minced basil; mix well and cool to room temperature.

In a large bowl, beat the egg yolks with ½ cup of the sugar until pale yellow and the mixture forms ribbons that slowly dissolve when the beaters are lifted. Add the chocolate mixture, hazelnuts, and flour; mix well.

Using clean, dry beaters, beat the egg whites until soft peaks form. Add the remaining ¼ cup sugar and beat until the whites are stiff but not dry. Gently fold one-third of the egg white mixture into the chocolate mixture. Fold in the remaining whites and mix gently.

Immediately pour batter into the prepared cake pans and bake in the center of oven for 35 minutes or until a toothpick inserted into the center of the cakes comes out clean. Cool cakes in pans on a wire rack. To serve, invert cakes from pans and cut into wedges. Garnish with the whipped cream and sprigs of basil.

To make a semisoft herbal soap: In a medium saucepan, add 2 cups of tightly packed basil leaves to 2 cups of boiling water. Cover, remove from the heat, and steep for 30 minutes. Strain, discarding the leaves. Place the herbal liquid in the top of a double boiler with enough water to make 1½ cups. Add about 1 cup (1 bar) of finely chopped Ivory soap; heat over a moderate flame, stirring frequently, until smooth and thickened. Pour into a wide-mouth container and cool to room temperature before using.

Index

Angel Hair Pasta with Lemon
   Basil, Asparagus, and Scallops, *43*

Baked Whole Snapper Stuffed
   with Cinnamon Basil and
   Onions, *51*

Basil
   about, *7-9*
   chiffonade, *15*
   chopping, *15*
   cooking of, *16*
   history, *7-8*
   mincing, *16*
   preparing, *15-16*
   purchasing, *10*
   pureeing, *16*
   storing, *13*
   varieties of, *11-13*

Burmese Coconut Chicken with
   Thai and Opal Basils, *45*

Chilled English Pea Soup with
   Lemon Basil, *32*

Chocolate-Hazelnut Torte with
   Cinnamon Basil, *64-65*

Cinnamon basil, *11*

Cinnamon Basil and Feta
   Cheese-stuffed New
   Potatoes, *20*

Cinnamon Basil and Goat
   Cheese Spread, *21*

Corn Chowder with Tomatoes
   and Basil, *30*

Corn Crab Cakes with Lemon
   Basil Mayonnaise, *27-28*

Crostini with Tomato, Basil,
   and Greek Cheese, *18*

Cucumber and Lemon Basil
   Yogurt Soup, *33*

Dark opal basil, *11*

Grilled Prawn Salad with
   Cinnamon Basil and Feta
   Cheese, *36*

Lemon basil, *12*

Lemon Basil Mayonnaise, *27*

Linguine with Basil, Walnuts, and Gorgonzola, *44*

Introduction, *7*

Onion, Fennel, and Goat Cheese Tart with Basil, *55-56*

Pan-fried Pork Tenderloin with Fennel, Sun-dried Tomatoes, and Basil, *50*

Poached Peaches with Cinnamon Basil Crème Frâiche, *59*

Poached Scallops with Deep-fried Basil, *40*

Pizzettas with Pesto and Assorted Toppings, *23-24*

Red Pepper Frittata with Basil, *25*

Roast Cornish Game Hen Stuffed with Two Basils, *46*

Roast Salmon with Corn and Lemon Basil Salad, *49*

Spiced Potato and Basil Gratin, *52*

Spiced Pound Cake with Lemon Basil-Orange Syrup, *60-61*

Spicy Vietnamese Mussel Salad with Thai Basil and Mint, *38-39*

Stir-fried Duck Breast with Cinnamon Basil and Ginger, *48*

Summer Berries and Figs with Honey-Basil Cream, *62*

Sweet basil, *13*

Thai basil, *11*

Thai Beef Curry with Anise and Two Basils, *53*

Thai Chicken and Eggplant Salad with Thai and Opal Basils, *34-35*

List of Recipes

APPETIZERS

Crostini with Tomato, Basil, and Greek Cheese	18
Cinnamon Basil-Feta Cheese-Stuffed New Potatoes	20
Cinnamon Basil-Goat Cheese Spread	21
Pizzettas with Pesto and Assorted Toppings	23
Red Pepper Frittata with Basil	25
Corn Crab Cakes with Lemon Basil Mayonnaise	27

SOUPS AND SALADS

Corn Chowder with Tomatoes and Basil	30
Chilled English Pea Soup with Lemon Basil	32
Cucumber-Lemon Basil Yogurt Soup	33
Thai Chicken and Eggplant Salad with Thai and Opal Basils	34
Grilled Prawn Salad with Cinnamon Basil and Feta Cheese	36
Spicy Vietmanese Mussel Salad with Thai Basil and Mint	38
Poached Scallops with Deep-fried Basil	40

ENTREES

Angel Hair Pasta with Lemon Basil, Asparagus, and Scallops	43
Linguine with Basil, Walnuts, and Gorgonzola	44
Burmese Coconut Chicken with Thai and Opal Basils	45
Roast Cornish Game Hens Stuffed with Two Basils	46
Stir-fried Duck Breast with Cinnamon Basil and Ginger	48

List of Recipes

ENTREES

Roast Salmon with Corn-Lemon Basil Salad   49

Pan-fried Pork Tenderloin with Fennel, Sun-dried Tomatoes, and Basil   50

Baked Whole Snapper Stuffed with Cinnamon Basil and Onions   51

Spiced Potato-Basil Gratin   52

Thai Beef Curry with Anise and Two Basils   53

Onion-Fennel and Goat Cheese Tart with Basil   55

DESSERTS

Poached Peaches with Cinnamon Basil Creme Fraiche   59

Spiced Pound Cake with Lemon Basil-Orange Syrup   60

Summer Berries and Figs with Honey-Basil Cream   62

Chocolate-Hazelnut Torte with Cinnamon Basil   64